ELVIS COSTELLO & ALLEN TOUSSAINT

THE RIVER IN REVERSE

ISBN-13: 978-1-4234-2007-1
ISBN-10: 1-4234-2007-1

HAL•LEONARD®
CORPORATION
7777 W. BLUEMOUND RD. P.O. BOX 13819 MILWAUKEE, WI 53213

Visit Hal Leonard Online at
www.halleonard.com

ON YOUR WAY DOWN

Words and Music by
ALLEN TOUSSAINT

Bluesy half-time feel

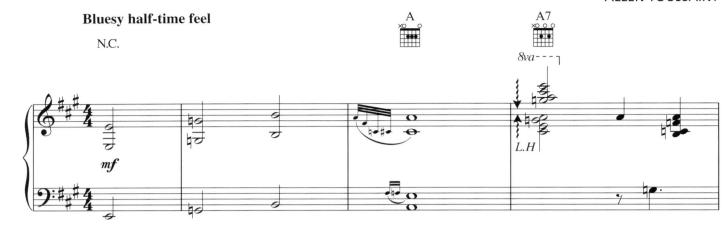

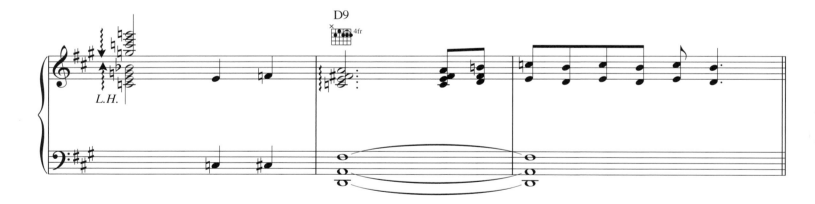

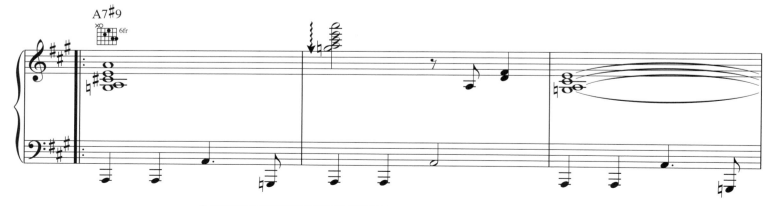

Think   the

NEARER TO YOU

Words and Music by
ALLEN TOUSSAINT

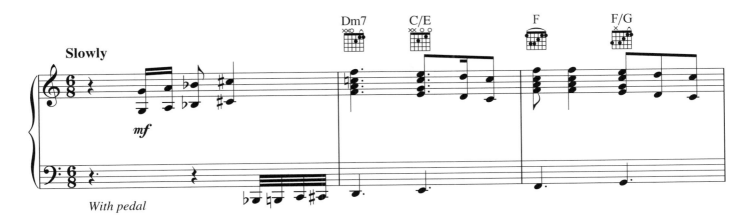

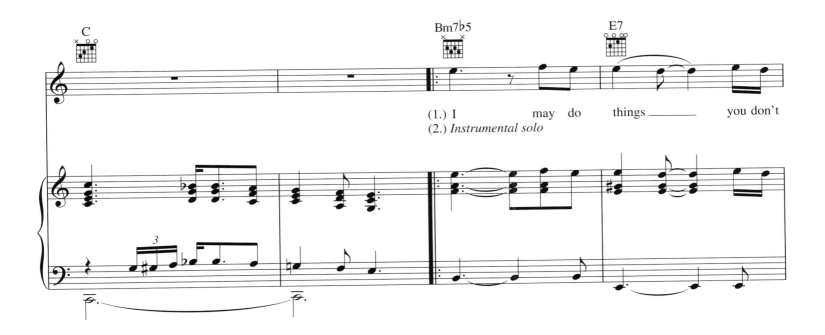

(1.) I may do things _____ you don't
(2.) *Instrumental solo*

un - der - stand, _____ but, re - mem - ber, I'm on - ly

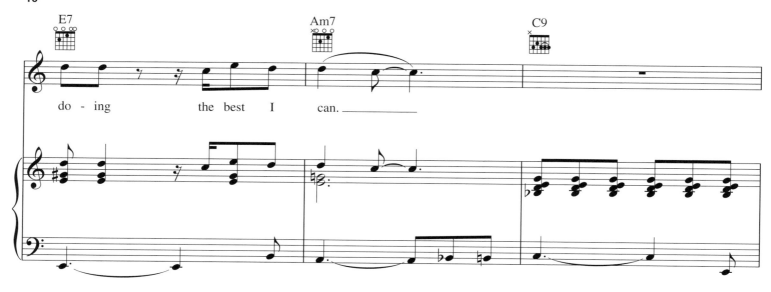

do - ing   the best I   can. _____

Ev - 'ry lit - tle thing I   do,   I'm tryin' to get   clos - er to
Solo ends Ev - 'ry deed __ I _____ do,   I'm tryin' to get   clos - er to

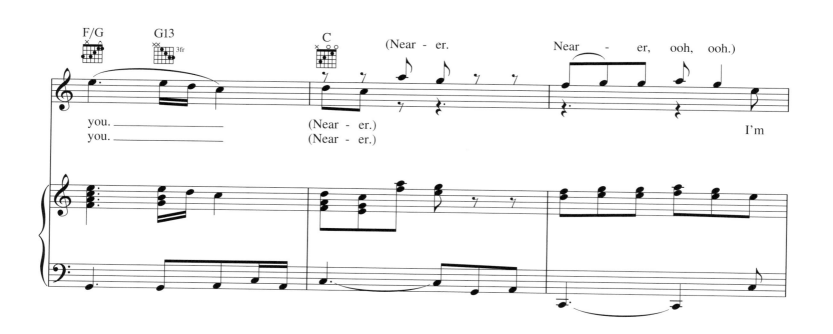

you. _____   (Near - er.)   (Near - er, ooh, ooh.)
you. _____   (Near - er.)   I'm

I've got to be near - er, near - er to you.

TEARS, TEARS AND MORE TEARS

Words and Music by
ALLEN TOUSSAINT

Fast Blues Rock

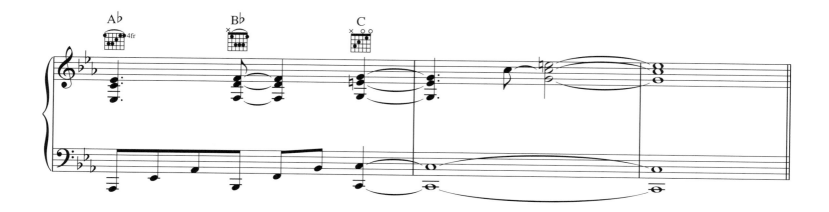

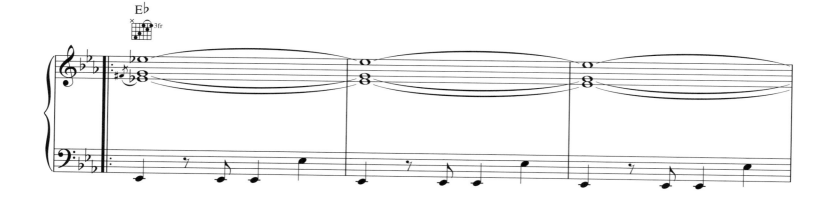

(1., D.S.) I

(D.S.) wake up ear - ly in the morn - ing; I
You did - n't say _____ what _____ hap - pened;

got you _____ on _____ my mind. _____
you just _____ walked _____ a - way. _____

E - ven a sim - ple phone __ call would suit __ me __ just
You've been noth - ing but sor - row and a lot of __ rain - y

fine. __ }
days. __ }

Tears, tears __ and more tears; { I can't __ oh

To Coda

help, but I keep on cry - ing, oh. __ }
ba - by, won't you please come home, __ oh? __ }

Tears, tears __ and

1

more tears; I can't __ get you off __ of my mind. __

more tears; oh, ___

___ you've been gone too long. ___ I re - mem - ber the

good times,   the good _____ times _____ we had. ___

How can you leave all that be - hind ___ like it was just an - oth - er place you had? __

Re - mem - ber the time ___ when we drank _
mem - ber the night ___ when I held ___

___ sweet wine? ___ I thought ev - er - y - thing ___ was fine. __
___ you tight ___ and let the world _____ pass ___ us by? __

- pened to the love we had, _____ oh? ____

Tears, tears __ and more tears; I got the blues, and I got them bad. __

more tears; ba - by, won't you please come home, _____ oh? __

Tears, tears __ and more tears; oh, _____ you've been gone too long. __

Repeat and Fade

Optional Ending

THE SHARPEST THORN

Words by ELVIS COSTELLO
and ALLEN TOUSSAINT
Music by ELVIS COSTELLO

WHO'S GONNA HELP BROTHER GET FURTHER?

Words and Music by
ALLEN TOUSSAINT

there's old John, __ two dol - lars in his pock - et, talk - ing loud and thinks he's rich. __

__ And look for lit - tle fool, too cool __ to go to school; get a

job, in two days __ he quits.   *Solo ends*   Pray tell, __ what's gon - na

hap - pen to broth - er?   Who's gon - na help him get fur - ther?   Huh, one an -

ding __ long.

yeah, _____ yeah. _____

Did it real-ly ding - dong? (Ding -

Repeat and Fade

dong.) It did - n't ding long.

Optional Ending

Did it real-ly

THE RIVER IN REVERSE

Words and Music by
ELVIS COSTELLO

How long does a prom-ise last? How long can a lie be told? _____

46

FREEDOM FOR THE STALLION

Words and Music by
ALLEN TOUSSAINT

BROKEN PROMISE LAND

Words by ELVIS COSTELLO
Music by ELVIS COSTELLO and ALLEN TOUSSAINT

There's a place _____ where words mean noth-ing
There's a town I know, _____ has a strange re-sem-blance to
There's a place _____ where in-fi-dels and ___

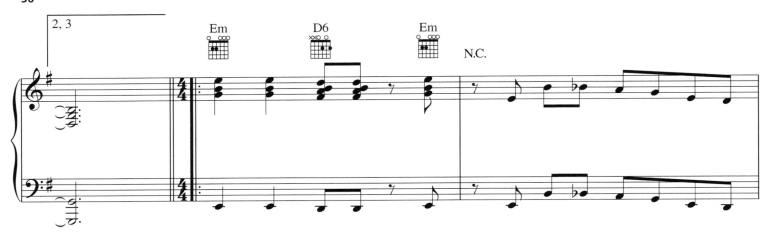

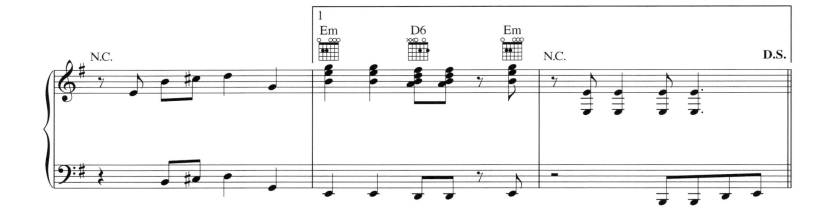

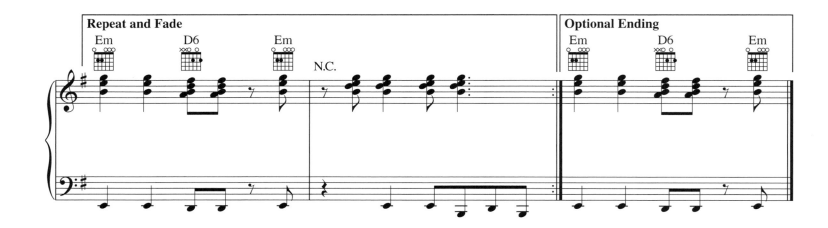

ASCENSION DAY

Words by ELVIS COSTELLO
Music by ALLEN TOUSSAINT and ROY BYRD

But we'll all _____ be to-geth - er

come As - cen - sion Day. _____

Piano solo

INTERNATIONAL ECHO

Words by ELVIS COSTELLO
Music by ALLEN TOUSSAINT

Moderate Rock

The

streets were de - sert - ed, and the house was dark. Down ___
Send out a mes - sage, and it's sure to re - bound. ___ What's ___
they paid me mon - ey for ___ playing pre - tend; then ___

67

their mark. In - ter - na - tion - al Ech - o.

Repeat and Fade

Optional Ending

All These Things

Words and Music by
ALLEN TOUSSAINT

WONDER WOMAN

Words and Music by
ALLEN TOUSSAINT

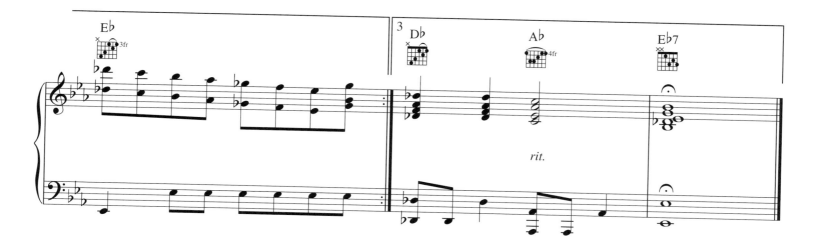

SIX-FINGERED MAN

Words by ELVIS COSTELLO
Music by ELVIS COSTELLO and ALLEN TOUSSAINT

Moderately slow

Six - fin - gered man, ___
Six - fin - gered man, ___
Six - fin - gered man, ___

play - ing a sev - en - string gui - tar. ___
al - ways the first to blow his horn. ___
shak - ing his fist at ev - 'ry - one. ___

There are Sev - en Dead - ly
His a - chieve - ments mul - ti -
Could - n't e - ven act his